SPORTS GREATS
TOP 10 TEAMS
IN FOOTBALL

DAVID ARETHA

Enslow Publishing
101 W. 23rd Street
Suite 240
New York, NY 10011
USA
enslow.com

Published in 2017 by Enslow Publishing, LLC.
101 W. 23rd Street, Suite 240, New York, NY 10011

Library of Congress Cataloging-in-Publication Data

Names: Aretha, David, author.
Title: Top 10 teams in football / David Aretha.
Other titles: Top 10 teams in football
Description: New York, NY : Enslow Publishing, 2017 | Series: Sports greats | Includes bibliographical references and index.
Identifiers: LCCN 2016024173| ISBN 9780766083103 (library bound) | ISBN 9780766083080 (pbk.) | ISBN 9780766083097 (6-pack)
Subjects: LCSH: Football team—United States—History—Juvenile literature.
Classification: LCC GV954 .A74 2017 | DDC 796.332/64—dc23
LC record available at https://lccn.loc.gov/2016024173

Printed in China

To Our Readers: We have done our best to make sure all website addresses in this book were active and appropriate when we went to press. However, the author and the publisher have no control over and assume no liability for the material available on those websites or on any websites they may link to. Any comments or suggestions can be sent by e-mail to customerservice@enslow.com.

Photo Credits: Cover, pp. 1, 12, 15, 21, 25, 33, 41 Focus On Sport/Getty Images; pp. 4-5, 43 Rob Tringali/Sportschrome/Getty Images; p. 9 Robert Riger/Hulton Archive/Getty Images; p. 11 Fred Kaplan / Sports Illustrated/Getty Images; pp. 17, 27 AP Photo/Al Messerschmidt; p. 19 Heinz Kluetmeier/Sports Illustrated/Getty Images; p. 23 Paul Natkin/Getty Images Sport/Getty Images; p. 29 Gin Ellis/Getty Images Sport/Getty Images; p. 31 Scott Cunningham/Getty Images Sport/Getty Images; p. 35 PAUL J. RICHARDS/AFP/Getty Images; p. 37 Bill Frakes/Sports Illustrated/Getty Images; p. 39 Kevin Reece/Getty Images Sport/Getty Images; p. 45 Kirby Lee/Getty Images Sport/Getty Images; design elements throughout book: maodoltee/Shutterstock.com (football field), RTimages/Shutterstock.com (grass), EsraKeskinSenay/Shutterstock.com (football stadium), Prixel Creative/Shutterstock.com (football play).

CONTENTS

INTRODUCTION

The New England Patriots (*left*) would have gone 19–0 in 2007...if it weren't for the New York Giants (*right*).

Can you name the eight undefeated teams in NFL history? If you can't, don't worry. We don't expect you to! Most of those teams played a long time ago. And besides, only one NFL team has had a perfect season.

In 1920, when the NFL was known as the American Professional Football Association, the Akron Pros went 8–0 with three ties. Coach Elgie Tobin's defense was so good that they allowed only seven points all year. But... they weren't exactly playing Tom Brady's New England Patriots. Akron's wins came against such teams as the Wheeling Stogies and Decatur Staleys. The league didn't even have play-off games until 1933.

The Canton Bulldogs went 21–0 with three ties in 1922–23, and the 1929 Green Bay Packers were 12–0 with a tie. But again, this was a simpler time. The 1922 Bulldogs were valued at $1,000. Compare that to today's Dallas Cowboys, who are worth approximately $4 billion!

The 1934 and 1942 Chicago Bears went undefeated with no ties during the regular season, but both seasons they lost in the NFL Championship Game. The 2007 Patriots were the only team to go 16–0 during a regular season. However, they lost to the New York Giants on a "miracle play" in the Super Bowl. Only the 1972 Dolphins have enjoyed a perfect NFL season. Under coach Don Shula, Miami won every regular season game that year (no ties) and stormed to victory in the Super Bowl.

The 1972 Dolphins and 2007 Patriots are among the ten top teams in NFL history. These ten clubs have certain things in common. All were coached by a tremendous leader, including such legends as Vince Lombardi, Chuck Noll, and Bill Belichick. These coaches thoroughly prepared for each game, and they made sure their players did, too. Said Lombardi, "You don't do things right once in a while...you do them right all the time."

These ten teams also featured a confident, highly effective leader at quarterback. Like generals in battle, quarterbacks Joe Montana, Terry Bradshaw, and Brett Favre marched their men down the field. These teams excelled in all phases of the game. Massive offensive linemen protected the quarterback and powered the running game. Speedy, hard-charging running backs (like Walter Payton and Franco Harris) found the end zone. So, too, did their dynamic, sticky-fingered receivers (Jerry Rice and Randy Moss to name a few). Powerful defensive units, such as Pittsburgh's "Steel Curtain," kept opponents off the board.

Besides great coaching and talent, these ten teams possessed a special quality: All of the players worked together toward a common goal. Assistant coach Bob Valesente of the 1996 Packers said his team possessed the four Cs: "chemistry, character, commitment, and competitiveness." Teammates became like family members, and together they fought their way to glory.

Now, let's take a closer look at the ten greatest football teams of all time!

1962 GREEN BAY PACKERS

COACH: VINCE LOMBARDI

RECORD: 13–1

POINTS SCORED: 415

POINTS ALLOWED: 148

POSTSEASON: WON NFL CHAMPIONSHIP GAME

"Winning isn't everything," Green Bay coach Vince Lombardi famously proclaimed, "it's the only thing." Clearly, the 1962 Packers got the message. Together, they went 13–1 and outscored their opponents by an average of 19.1 points per game—the largest margin in NFL history.

Lombardi—the league's greatest coach ever, according to ESPN—joined the Packers in 1959. At the first day of each training camp, he said to his players, "Gentlemen, *this* is a football." He and his staff then taught all of the game's fundamentals. Throughout the season, Lombardi demanded maximum dedication.

From 1961 to 1967, Green Bay won the league championship five times—including the first two Super Bowls. The 1962 season stands out as a diamond among the jewels. The Packers won all six of their preseason games and kept on rolling.

Incredibly, the 1962 team featured ten future Hall of Famers. On offense, quarterback Bart Starr, halfback Paul Hornung, center Jim Ringo, and right tackle Forrest Gregg would all be enshrined. So, too, would fullback Jim Taylor, who in 1962 led the NFL in touchdowns (19) and rushing yards (1,474).

Linebacker Ray Nitschke, once an anger-filled orphan, focused his aggression on opponents. He was so tough that when a fifteen-foot iron tower fell on him one day, Lombardi was unconcerned. He knew Nitschke was indestructible. Four other Packers defenders would join Nitschke in the Hall of Fame: cornerback Herb Adderley, defensive end Willie Davis, safety Willie Wood, and defensive tackle Henry Jordan.

Green Bay opened the regular season with ten straight victories. One of those wins was a 49–0 annihilation of Philadelphia. The Packers amassed 37 first downs and outgained the Eagles 628 yards to 54!

Green Bay's only loss came on Thanksgiving Day in Detroit, where the Lions prevailed 26–14. In a way, Lombardi was grateful for this lesson in humility. "From now on, we'll be a lot better ball club for it," he said before his turkey dinner. The Packers responded with a 41–10 drubbing of the Los Angeles Rams. They then beat San Francisco 31–21 and the Rams 20–17. "We're a tired ball club," Lombardi said after the last game, "a very tired ball club."

In the 1962 NFL Championship Game, the Packers blew the Giants out of Yankee Stadium, winning 16–7.

All of that dominating had worn them out. The Packers set a still-standing NFL record with 36 rushing touchdowns, and they led the league with 31 interceptions.

Back then, the play-offs consisted of one contest: the NFL Championship Game. On a frigid day in 1962, the New York Giants hosted the Packers at Yankee Stadium. It was so windy, the sideline benches "actually blew over and onto the field during the game," Starr wrote in *The First America's Team*. He added that, "I didn't have the arm strength and accuracy to deal with those conditions." So, Taylor ran the ball 31 times, crashing each time on a rock-hard field. He scored a touchdown, Jerry Kramer booted three short field goals, and the defense held the Giants to 7 points.

The Packers then flew back to Green Bay. At the airport, ten thousand fans greeted the greatest team that they—or anyone—had ever seen.

1972 MIAMI DOLPHINS
Coach: Don Shula
Record: 14–0
Points Scored: 385
Points Allowed: 171
Postseason: Won Super Bowl

In January 1972, moments after Miami lost to Dallas in the Super Bowl, coach Don Shula addressed his players.

"We all hurt right now," Shula said. "It's painful. It stings. But I don't want you to forget how this feels. Take it with you everywhere. Remember it now and when you leave here...Remember it next season. Remember it so when we get back to the Super Bowl next year, the highs of winning it will feel even greater."

Later, Dolphins running back Larry Csonka revealed something else Shula said about the 1972 season: "We're gonna win every game." And sure enough, they did.

The 1972 Dolphins are the only team in NFL history to go undefeated—14–0 in the regular season and 3–0 in the play-offs. The head coach deserved much of the credit. Demanding perfection in all aspects of the game, Shula had gone 71–23–4 as the Baltimore Colts head coach from 1963 to 1969. In his first season with Miami

Composed head coach Don Shula (in blue) talks to quarterback Bob Griese during the 1972 AFC Championship Game. Two Jim Kiick touchdown runs in the second half led to a 21–17 Dolphins victory.

in 1970, he turned a previously lousy Dolphins team into a 10–4 club. The next year, they went 10–3–1.

The 1972 Dolphins featured a balanced offense. That year, Miami became the first NFL team ever with two 1,000-yard rushers. Csonka hammered his way to 1,117 yards, and speedy Mercury Morris dashed to an even 1,000. Quarterback Bob Griese, First Team All-Pro a year earlier, started just five games in 1972 due to injury. Earl Morrall, age thirty-eight, filled in capably. His favorite target: lightning-quick wide receiver Paul Warfield, who averaged 20.9 yards per catch.

The Dolphins led the NFL in points and yards, *and* they allowed the fewest points and yards. Their "No-Name Defense" actually sent two players to the Pro Bowl. One was linebacker Nick Buoniconti, who hit surprisingly hard for a 5-foot-11, 220-pounder. The other was defensive end Bill Stanfill, who "combined speed, size, range, quickness and competitiveness," said his college coach, Vince Dooley.

The speedy Mercury Morris follows blockers during the Super Bowl against Washington. Miami's defense was the story of the game. The Dolphins won 14–7, with the Redskins' touchdown coming on a fumble return.

The Dolphins had only two scares during the regular season. At Minnesota, they overcame a 14–6 fourth-quarter deficit. Garo Yepremian booted a 51-yard field goal (super-long for that era), and Griese won the game with a touchdown pass to Jim Mandich. Against the New York Jets, Morris scored on a 14-yard run in the fourth quarter to win the game, 28–24. Miami also breezed to easy victories over New England (52–0) and Baltimore twice (23–0 and 16–0).

In the play-offs, the Dolphins earned hard-fought victories over Cleveland (20–14) and Pittsburgh (21–17). The Washington Redskins were actually favored to win the Super Bowl, but Griese led the Dolphins to a 14–0 lead. Then, in the fourth quarter, the 'Skins took advantage of one of the biggest blunders in NFL history.

With 2:38 remaining, Yepremian's field goal attempt was blocked, but the ball popped up and landed in his hands. He then ran backward and tried to throw the pigskin, but it slipped out of his hand and shot straight up into the air. He then batted the ball…right to Washington's Mike Bass. Bass took it 49 yards for a touchdown, and the extra point made it 14–7.

With 1:14 remaining, Washington got the ball back. But the Dolphins sacked quarterback Billy Kilmer on fourth down, ending the game.

A year later, the Dolphins approached perfection again. They went 12–2 and won another Super Bowl.

1978 PITTSBURGH STEELERS
COACH: CHUCK NOLL

RECORD: 14–2

POINTS SCORED: 356

POINTS ALLOWED: 195

POSTSEASON: WON SUPER BOWL

Prior to the 1978 season's Super Bowl, Steelers quarterback Terry Bradshaw heard a nasty comment about his intelligence. Dallas linebacker Hollywood Henderson said that Bradshaw couldn't spell "cat" if you gave him the *c* and the *t*. As a student in Louisiana, Bradshaw wrote in his autobiography, "I believed I just wasn't as smart as the other kids." But he was plenty smart on the football field. Bradshaw led Pittsburgh to four Super Bowl victories in one decade—a claim that no other human being can make.

The 1970s Steelers are perhaps the greatest dynasty in football history. They won the Super Bowl during the 1974, 1975, 1978, and 1979 seasons, and the 1978 team was the best of the bunch. That year, Bradshaw threw to two future Hall of Fame receivers: the acrobatic Lynn Swann and the ultra-reliable John Stallworth. Meanwhile, Franco Harris topped 1,000 yards rushing for the sixth time. Teammate Joe Greene remembered

With Hollywood Henderson on the ground, Terry Bradshaw zips a pass against Dallas in the Super Bowl. Bradshaw completed 17 tosses for 318 yards.

the big, rugged Harris as the guy who "got us that rough first down...the guy the team rallied around."

Coached by the calm, cerebral Chuck Noll, the 1978 Steelers sent ten players to the Pro Bowl. "Mean" Joe Greene, Dwight "Mad Dog" White, Ernie "Fats" Holmes, and L. C. Greenwood (with his gold shoes) formed the legendary "Steel Curtain" defensive line. Jack Lambert, known as "Count Dracula in Cleats," teamed with fellow future Hall of Fame linebacker Jack Ham. Future Hall of Fame cornerback Mel Blount "was the most incredible athlete I have ever seen," Ham said.

"With Mel, you could take one wide receiver and just write him off."

The 1978 Steelers held their opponents to just 12.2 points per game — the lowest mark in the league. The team started 7–0 and finished 14–2.

With their fans waving yellow "Terrible Towels," Pittsburgh rolled through the postseason. They cruised by Denver 33–10 before hosting the AFC Championship Game. On a cold, rainy day at Three Rivers Stadium, the Steelers iced Houston 34–5. The Oilers fumbled the ball four times, and Pittsburgh picked off five Dan Pastorini passes.

Henderson made his bullying remark prior to the Super Bowl in Miami. Bradshaw responded by throwing three touchdown passes in the first half. Two went to Stallworth, including a crowd-rousing 75-yarder. By halftime, Bradshaw had broken Bart Starr's Super Bowl full-game record of 250 passing yards.

In the fourth quarter, Henderson added a *physical* cheap shot to his verbal one: he sacked Bradshaw after the play had been whistled dead. That made Franco Harris angry. On the next play, Harris powered his way to a 22-yard touchdown. "I've never seen him run so hard...," Bradshaw said. "He'd run through a brick wall if the brick wall would have kept him out of the end zone."

That touchdown and the extra point made it 28–17, and Bradshaw threw his fourth touchdown pass — to

Swann—to give Pittsburgh a 35–17 lead. Behind "Captain Comeback," quarterback Roger Staubach, Dallas cut the lead to 35–31. But the Steelers held on for the victory.

Bradshaw finished with 318 passing yards and was named the game's MVP—which, Mr. Henderson, he had no trouble spelling.

Four future Hall of Famers celebrate during the Super Bowl. They include, from left to right, running back Franco Harris, wide receiver Lynn Swann, quarterback Terry Bradshaw, and center Mike Webster.

1984 SAN FRANCISCO 49ERS

COACH: BILL WALSH

RECORD: 15–1

POINTS SCORED: 475

POINTS ALLOWED: 227

POSTSEASON: WON SUPER BOWL

It was a warm, sunny October day in San Francisco, and nervous fans were on their feet. With one short kick, the 49ers could go to overtime. If Ray Wersching could successfully boot a 37-yard field goal, San Francisco would tie Pittsburgh at 20–20. But… Wersching's kick sailed wide, and the clock expired.

On that day in 1984, the 49ers fell to 6–1. It was the only loss of their entire season.

Under brilliant head coach Bill Walsh, the 1981 Niners won the Super Bowl. They entered 1984 as the overwhelming favorite to win it again. "I remember the 49ers always seemed to come out on top," said Ahmed Plummer, who would play for the team years later. "They were like the Little League team you could never beat."

On offense, Walsh had developed a system that drove defenders crazy. The 49ers threw the ball half the time and ran it half the time, meaning foes didn't know what was coming. He also installed a large number of sophisticated plays to keep defenses guessing. Legendary quarterback Joe Montana fired the ball with laser-like accuracy—and he threw it to everybody. Wide receivers Dwight Clark and Freddic Solomon, tight end Earl Cooper, and running back Roger Craig all caught at least 40 passes in 1984.

While linebackers kept their eyes on potential receivers, the Niners ran the ball up the gut. Wendell Tyler (1,262 rushing yards) led an offense that ranked second in the NFL with 4.6 yards per carry. On defense, San Francisco's Dwaine Board led the team with 10 sacks, and linebacker Keena Turner

Joe Montana (*left*) spread his passes around in 1984. Running back Roger Craig (*right*) made 71 receptions. The next year, Craig would top 1,000 yards rushing and 1,000 yards receiving.

was named to the Pro Bowl. So, too, were defensive backs Dwight Hicks, Carlton Williamson, and future Hall of Famer Ronnie Lott.

After the loss to Pittsburgh, San Francisco began blowing out opponents. They defeated the Los Angeles Rams 33–0, Cleveland 41–7, New Orleans 35–3, and Minnesota 51–7. "That team had so much chemistry," said Hicks. "We were a very confident group of players, and believed in each other. And I believe that's why we were so successful."

In the play-offs, Montana threw two early touchdown passes in a 21–10 win over the New York Giants. In the NFC Championship Game, the Niners steamrolled the Chicago Bears. San Francisco's defense sacked quarterback Steve Fuller eight times and held him to 87 yards passing.

The Super Bowl pitted two of the greatest quarterbacks in NFL history: Montana and the Miami Dolphins' Dan Marino. That year Miami went 14–2, as Marino became the first NFL quarterback to throw for 5,000 yards in a season.

Fans expected a high-scoring affair, and they got it—but only from the 49ers. Montana fired three touchdown passes and ran for another score. Meanwhile, San Francisco's ferocious defense intercepted Marino twice and sacked him four times. The Niners led 28–10 in the second quarter and breezed to a 38–16 victory.

"Coach Walsh," said President Ronald Reagan after the game, "there ought to be a bigger word for *congratulations* for all that we saw tonight and what you and that team of yours have accomplished."

"Well, I tell ya," Walsh replied, "they've given it all year, Mr. President. This is the greatest football team... I've ever been around."

A year later, a coach from Chicago could make that same claim.

1985 CHICAGO BEARS

COACH: MIKE DITKA

RECORD: 15–1

POINTS SCORED: 456

POINTS ALLOWED: 198

POSTSEASON: WON SUPER BOWL

It had seemed like *forever* since a Chicago sports team had won a championship. So when the Bears roared to a 12–0 start in 1985, it was time to celebrate. On December 3—one day after their only loss of the season—twenty-four Bears recorded "The Super Bowl Shuffle." The song and the video became national hits.

Ten of the most prominent players rapped during the song. Singers included quarterback Jim McMahon in his sunglasses ("I'm the punky QB") and legendary running back Walter Payton, known as "Sweetness." Feared middle linebacker Mike Singletary rapped, "I'm Samurai Mike. I stop 'em cold." And defensive end Richard Dent warned that the "sackman's coming." (He totaled 17 sacks that year.) Even rookie William "Refrigerator" Perry got to rap. The 335-pounder lined up at defensive tackle, but he also played a little running back that year.

Wide receiver Willie Gault (83) and rookie William "Refrigerator" Perry (72) were among the Bears who performed "The Super Bowl Shuffle."

When "the Fridge" rushed for a touchdown on *Monday Night Football*, fans went berserk.

Bears head coach "Iron Mike" Ditka took on god-like status in Chicago. Fans loved "Da Coach" for his toughness, mustache, gum chewing, aviator sunglasses, and frank talk. He once formed his thumb and index finger into a "zero" and said to a reporter, "Yo, buddy. Here's your IQ!"

Disciplined but free-spirited, the 1985 Bears ranked second in the NFL in scoring and first in fewest points allowed. Payton glided to 1,551 rushing yards as a First Team All-Pro. Six players on the legendary defense made the Pro Bowl: Singletary, Dent, linebacker Otis Wilson, strong safety Dave Duerson, and linemen Dan Hampton and Steve McMichael. Singletary, who captained the defense, could see plays developing with his great field vision eyes. "On defense he is the glue," said McMahon. "When he talks, people listen."

After a 5–0 start, the Bears' defense really kicked in. They defeated reigning champion San Francisco 26–10 by sacking Joe Montana seven times. Chicago won the next six games by scores of 23–7, 27–9, 16–10, 24–3, 44–0, and 36–0. The 16–10 triumph over Green Bay came after the Packers put horse manure in the Bears' locker room.

Chicago lost in Miami, 38–24, on a Monday night to fall to 12–1. Three easy victories followed, and they entered the play-offs at 15–1.

The Bears opened the postseason by crushing the Giants 21–0 on a brutally cold Chicago afternoon. New York rushed for just 32 yards, while quarterback Phil Simms was sacked six times for minus-60 yards. In the NFC Championship Game, the Bears destroyed the Los Angeles Rams 24–0. They capped the scoring with a sack/fumble; Wilber Marshall scooped it up and ran 52 yards for a touchdown.

Down in New Orleans for Super Bowl XX, New England scored first to make it 3–0. The Bears responded with 44 points in a row. Three field goals and three touchdown runs (two by McMahon) made it 30–3.

Then the real fun began. Reggie Phillips intercepted a pass and returned it 28 yards for a touchdown. The Fridge, lining up in the backfield, blasted in for a touchdown and then spiked the daylights out of the ball. Henry Waechter capped the scoring at 46–10 when he sacked New England's Steve Grogan in the end zone.

Due to Chicago's 15–1 record and utter dominance in the postseason, ESPN voted the 1985 Bears the greatest team in NFL history.

1989 SAN FRANCISCO 49ERS

COACH: GEORGE SEIFERT

RECORD: 14–2

POINTS SCORED: 442

POINTS ALLOWED: 253

POSTSEASON: WON SUPER BOWL

Joe Montana could feel his age. On September 24, 1989, the Philadelphia Eagles sacked the thirty-three-year-old 49ers quarterback six times in the first half. "Joe Cool" had been the greatest quarterback of the 1980s, but perhaps he was falling into decline. In San Francisco, fans sighed as the Eagles moved ahead 28–10 in the fourth quarter...But then it happened.

Like a shining knight on a white horse, ol' Joe took the field by storm. In a span of 14 plays, Montana fired touchdown passes to John Taylor (70 yards), Tom Rathman (8), Brent Jones (25), and superstar Jerry Rice (33). On that day, he threw for 428 yards and 5 TDs, as San Francisco roared to a 38–28 victory.

"It's been written many times about Joe's ability to come back," said San Francisco's first-year head coach, George Seifert. "You saw it happen again today. His cool under pressure is amazing."

The 1989 Niners ranked third in the NFL in fewest points allowed. They also could run the football, with Roger Craig rushing for 1,054 yards. But the efficiency of the passing game is what really made San Francisco special.

On the year, Montana set an NFL record with a passer rating of 112.4. That calculation factors in the quarterback's completion percentage, number of completions, passing yards, touchdown passes, and interceptions. Montana completed 70.2 percent of his passes — nearly an NFL record. He tallied 26 touchdown passes compared to just 8 interceptions.

Wide receiver Jerry Rice breezes to one of his three touchdowns against Denver in the Super Bowl. In 2010, a panel of NFL experts voted Rice the greatest player in league history.

Wide receivers Jerry Rice and John Taylor both topped 1,000 receiving yards, and Craig caught 73 passes out of the backfield. Even backup quarterback Steve Young got into the act, throwing for 1,001 yards. The 49ers led the league in points and yardage, and Montana won the NFL MVP Award.

A devastating earthquake shook the San Francisco area in October. But in subsequent weeks, the Niners brought some joy back to the city—especially on a Monday night in December. At Los Angeles, the 49ers turned two fourth-quarter Rams fumbles into touchdowns. They scored the last 20 points to win 30–27, with Montana throwing for 458 yards.

San Francisco closed the season at 14–2 after a 26–0 drubbing of Chicago. That was a prelude to their play-off dominance. In the three postseason games, Montana completed 78.3 percent of his passes for 800 yards, 11 touchdowns, and no interceptions. His passer rating was through the roof: 146.4.

First, they routed Minnesota 41–13, with Montana throwing four first half touchdown passes. "Winning like that takes the excitement out of it," Joe said. Then they blew away the Rams 30–3, with Montana completing 26 of 30 tosses. "Obviously we were overwhelmed," said Rams coach John Robinson.

Down in New Orleans, San Francisco entered the Super Bowl as a 13-point favorite over Denver. They won by 45 points, 55–10. Montana completed 22 of 29 for 297 yards and five touchdowns, including three to Rice. It remains the biggest rout in Super Bowl history, and it all happened because of their "aging" QB. "He's probably the greatest quarterback ever to play the game," Seifert said afterward. "Everybody rallies behind him. We all have an inner strength because of his strength."

San Francisco's offensive line allows quarterback Joe Montana time to do his thing. The 49ers' 55 points that day set a Super Bowl record that still stands.

1991 WASHINGTON REDSKINS
COACH: JOE GIBBS
RECORD: 14–2
POINTS SCORED: 485
POINTS ALLOWED: 224
POSTSEASON: WON SUPER BOWL

When fans talk about the greatest NFL team of all time, few remember the 1991 Redskins. Washington didn't have a perfect record, like the 1972 Dolphins. They didn't make a music video, like the 1985 Bears. But, wrote Aaron Schatz of FootballOutsiders .com, "Washington may have been the most well-rounded team in NFL history."

It all started with "the Hogs," the team's offensive line. Led by tackles Jim Lachey and Joe Jacoby, the Hogs yielded only 9 sacks the whole season. They allowed slow-footed quarterback Mark Rypien to take his time and throw 28 touchdown passes—second most in the league. They helped workhorse Earnest Byner, elusive Ricky Ervins, and powerful Gerald Riggs to rush for nearly 2,000 yards.

"The Hogs were our engine," said kick returner Brian Mitchell. "They made everything go."

The Redskins opened the season with a 45–0 blowout of Detroit, and later in September they shut out Phoenix 34–0 and Philadelphia 23–0. Following 56–17 and 41–14 routs in November, they were 11–0.

The Redskins lacked superstars. But, said John McDonnell of the *Washington Post,* "Everybody, on a scale of 1 to 10, played like an 8 ½ or a 9 all the

Left tackle Jim Lachey was the best of Washington's offensive linemen, known as "the Hogs." In 1991, the Associated Press named Lachey a First Team All-Pro.

time." Wide receivers Gary Clark and Art Monk each topped 1,000 receiving yards. Mitchell returned two punts for touchdowns. Kicker Chip Lohmiller made the Pro Bowl.

The Redskins ranked first in the league in scoring and second in fewest points allowed. Linebackers Andre Collins and Wilber Marshall combined for over 280 tackles. Charles Mann recorded 11.5 of the team's 50 sacks. Cornerback Darrell Green made First Team All-Pro—the only Redskin to do so.

Washington faced an especially difficult schedule, yet they almost went 16–0. They fell to 11–1 after a 24–21 loss at home to Dallas. They improved to 14–1 before playing a meaningless game at season's end. Having already clinched home field advantage throughout the play-offs, they rested their starters and lost to Philadelphia 24–22.

Washington's postseason games were so lopsided that fans had to find ways to entertain themselves. The Redskins opened the play-offs with a 24–7 rout of Atlanta in a driving rainstorm. The fans, who were given gold seat cushions before the game, flung them onto the field after it was over. It was "Rainin' Cats, Dogs and Seat Cushions," proclaimed the *Washington Post*.

Detroit had its best team in decades, but the Redskins annihilated the Lions 41–10. They held Barry Sanders, perhaps the greatest running back ever, to just 44 yards.

Prior to the Super Bowl against Buffalo, the Bills defensive line coach disrespected the Hogs. "They're all old," Washington tight end Don Warren recalled him

Members of the Washington offense flash thumbs-up signs during the Super Bowl. Including the play-offs, the Redskins outscored opponents by 322 points that season.

saying. "They're not any good. They're big and fat now." Those words served as motivation. The Hogs helped the Redskins take a 24–0 lead in the third quarter, and they cruised to 37–24. Game MVP Rypien threw for 292 yards, and not once did the Hogs allow a sack. Green credited the success to "a good variety of things in our game plan…It was like a pizza with olives and onions and green peppers and everything you can think of. We dished it out with everything we had."

Years later, Mitchell reflected on the 1991 Redskins. "From top to bottom—offense, defense, special teams— we were special," he said. "That's the word: special."

1996 GREEN BAY PACKERS

COACH: MIKE HOLMGREN

RECORD: 13–3

POINTS SCORED: 456

POINTS ALLOWED: 210

POSTSEASON: WON SUPER BOWL

For the 1996 Packers, the excitement began in early September. Green Bay opened the season with a 34–3 crushing of Tampa Bay, and a day later President Bill Clinton visited the team at Lambeau Field. Wide receiver/rapper Robert Brooks handed the president a copy of his CD, *Jump into the Stands*. The following Monday, Brooks did just that. After both of his touchdown receptions that night, he took a "Lambeau Leap" into the seats. Packers fans patted Brooks and then cheered their team to victory. They crushed Philadelphia 39–13.

The little city of Green Bay, Wisconsin, was starving for a championship. Its team hadn't won a championship since Super Bowl II in 1968. But with the emergence of quarterback Brett Favre and a dynamite defense, the Pack made it to the NFC Championship Game in 1995. A year later, they looked to go all the way.

Head coach Mike Holmgren wore a glum expression under his mustache, but he knew how to motivate his men. The Packers were known for their great team play, with everyone working toward a common goal. And they had quarterback Brett Favre. The NFL MVP in 1995 and 1996, Favre played with fire and pizzazz. In 1996, he led the NFL with 39 touchdown passes.

Green Bay did lose three games in 1996, but in their wins they were amazing. They became the first team since the legendary 1972 Dolphins to lead the NFL in both points scored and fewest points allowed.

President Bill Clinton (red tie) inspires the Packers during a visit on Labor Day. After the season, they would all meet again at the White House, where Clinton honored the Super Bowl champions.

Reggie White (the "Minister of Defense") and First Team All-Pro LeRoy Butler led a ferocious defense. They allowed just 12 touchdown passes all year while recording 26 interceptions. Dynamic kick returner Desmond Howard helped the team set an NFL record for punt return yardage.

Following a 21–6 Monday night loss at Dallas, the Packers fell to 8–3. But in their eight remaining games, including the postseason, they won every contest by a large margin. They closed the regular season with a 41–6 victory over Denver, a 31–3 rout of Detroit, and a 38–10 pasting of the Vikings. In December, *Sports Illustrated* featured Favre on the cover with the headline "The Team to Beat."

In the magazine's cover story, wide receiver Andre Rison said, "the vibe here is incredible." Defensive tackle Santana Dotson added that, "everyone from the front office executives to the janitor tries to get the players whatever they need to win."

Known affectionately as "Cheeseheads" (because Wisconsin makes a lot of cheese), Packers fans went wild during the play-offs. Against San Francisco at Lambeau, Howard opened the scoring with a 71-yard punt return for a touchdown. The Packers won on a muddy field 35–14. Then next week, amid a wind chill of -16 degrees, they clobbered Carolina 30–13.

In the Super Bowl against New England, Favre found Rison wide open for a 54-yard touchdown pass to open the scoring. The Patriots stayed close throughout the game, but they couldn't contain Howard. He had punt returns of 32 and 34 yards, and his 99-yard kickoff return ended the scoring. "That one play killed us," said New England's Ray Lucas. Green Bay prevailed 35–21, and Howard was named Super Bowl MVP.

The Packers may have had three losses. But in 2007, ESPN ranked them the sixth greatest Super Bowl team of all time.

Desmond Howard (*right*) would return this kickoff for a touchdown against New England in the Super Bowl. Howard returned 10 kicks (kickoffs and punts) for 244 yards in the game.

1999 ST. LOUIS RAMS
COACH: DICK VERMEIL
RECORD: 13–3
POINTS SCORED: 526
POINTS ALLOWED: 242
POSTSEASON: WON SUPER BOWL

S tep right up, folks, and witness the "the Greatest Show on Turf!"

That's what they called the offense of the 1999 St. Louis Rams. St. Louis ran a system in which five guys often went out for a pass. Quarterback Kurt Warner orchestrated this aerial attack. He led the team to 526 points, second-most ever by an NFL team at the time. He paced the league in touchdown passes (41), completion percentage (65.1), and passer rating (109.2). Warner even earned the NFL MVP Award that year— pretty incredible considering that just five years earlier, he was making $5.50 an hour at a grocery store.

Kurt Warner is football's ultimate rags-to-riches story. After playing at the tiny University of Northern Iowa, the handsome QB went undrafted in 1994. He tried out for the Green Bay Packers but got cut.

Without work, he moved in with his girlfriend's parents and got a job stocking shelves at Hy-Vee in Cedar Rapids, Iowa. The next year he signed with the Iowa Barnstormers of the Arena Football League, where he developed into a touchdown-passing machine. He starred in a European league in 1998 and entered 1999 as the Rams' backup quarterback.

When starting QB Trent Green fell to injury in the 1999 preseason, the Rams were forced to go with Warner. "Everybody was scared about the quarterback position, and I mean everybody,

In three postseason games following the 1999 campaign, Kurt Warner threw for 391, 258, and 414 yards.

except for Kurt," said teammate D'Marco Farr. Showing confidence and a rocket arm, Warner threw three touchdown passes in each of his first three games. The following week, he fired five TD passes against San Francisco. "And you know what he told me walking off the field today?" said feisty head coach Dick Vermeil. "He said, 'You haven't seen the best of it yet.'"

Warner was fortunate to share the backfield with running back Marshall Faulk. "Faulk possesses blinding acceleration, quickness, speed and toughness," wrote Thomas George in the *New York Times*. In 1998, Faulk rushed for 1,381 yards and caught 87 passes for 1,048 yards. Warner also favored speedy Pro Bowl wide receiver Isaac Bruce, who amassed 1,165 receiving yards and 12 touchdowns.

The Rams' defense ranked fourth in the NFL in fewest points allowed. Defensive end Kevin Carter—a 290-pound terror—led the league with 17 sacks. Still, the offense powered this team. The Rams scored at least 30 points in 12 of their 16 games.

In the play-offs, the Rams defeated Minnesota 49–37 (with Warner throwing for 5 touchdowns) and Tampa Bay 11–6. They then battled Tennessee in one of the most exciting Super Bowls of all time.

After St. Louis went ahead 16–0, the Titans tied the score at 16–16 with 2:12 left in the game. On the next play, the Rams lined up with four wide receivers and sent

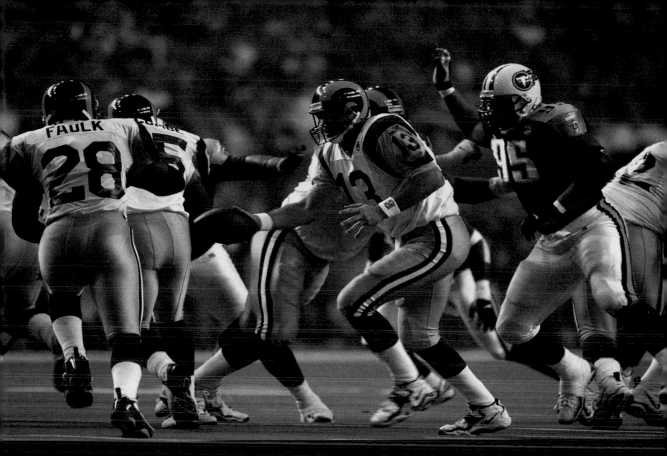

Marshall Faulk gets the carry against Tennessee in the Super Bowl. Kurt Warner's 73-yard touchdown pass to Isaac Bruce with 1:54 remaining proved to be the winning score.

them all downfield. Warner fired deep down the left sideline to Bruce, who caught the ball and then blasted into the end zone. Down 23–16, the Titans stormed back. With five seconds left, they had the ball at the Rams' 10-yard line. Steve McNair then completed a pass to Kevin Dyson, but linebacker Mike Jones tackled him at the 1-yard line as time expired.

Warner, the game's MVP, set a Super Bowl record with 414 passing yards. "I guess it is sort of a storybook ending," he said. No kidding.

2007 NEW ENGLAND PATRIOTS

COACH: BILL BELICHICK

RECORD: 16–0

POINTS SCORED: 589

POINTS ALLOWED: 274

POSTSEASON: LOST SUPER BOWL

Ellis Hobbs was feeling lucky. It was the 2007 season opener against the Jets—a hot day in New York. Hobbs caught the kickoff 8 yards deep in the end zone. He should have taken a knee, but instead he returned the kickoff 108 yards for a touchdown.

Hobbs's return set the tone for the most amazing season any NFL team has ever had. The Patriots became the first NFL club to go 16–0, then lost the Super Bowl on a miracle play by the New York Giants.

Bill Belichick was a serious guy who mumbled to the press. He was also the premier coach in the league, having won three Super Bowls in the 2000s. In 2007, he and superstar quarterback Tom Brady welcomed two new wide receivers. Tiny Wes Welker would lead the NFL with 112 catches in 2007. The spectacular

Randy Moss was quarterback Tom Brady's favorite target in 2007. His 1,483 receiving yards ranked second in the NFL, and his 23 touchdown catches set a league record.

Randy Moss would set the league record with 23 touchdown receptions.

Incredibly, the Patriots opened 2007 with eight blowout victories: 38–14, 38–14, 38–7, 34–13, 34–17, 48–27, 49–28, and 52–7. Unbelievably, Brady threw 30 touchdown passes and just 2 interceptions in the season's first half. The next week they traveled to Indianapolis to face the 7–0 Colts, quarterbacked by the great Peyton Manning. Down 20–10 in the fourth quarter, Brady fired two late touchdown passes to win the game. While Patriots fans were ecstatic, Belichick remained unemotional and focused. "This was just a football game against the Colts," he said. "That's all it was."

The Patriots followed with a 56–10 romp over Buffalo, then defeated Philadelphia and Baltimore on fourth-quarter comebacks. They cruised in their remaining games to reach regular-season perfection. The Patriots' 589 points and 75 touchdowns set NFL records, as did their 315-point differential. Brady, the NFL MVP, set a league record with 50 TD passes. First Team All-Pro linebacker Mike Vrabel (12.5 sacks) led a defense that finished fourth in the league in fewest yards allowed.

In the play-offs, New England defeated Jacksonville 31–20 and San Diego 21–12 to advance to the Super Bowl. There they faced the New York Giants, who had gone 10–6 during the regular season. Quarterbacked by Eli Manning—Peyton's younger brother—the Giants were 13.5-point underdogs. The Patriots, it seemed, would have no trouble becoming the NFL's first 19–0 team. Or so everyone thought.

With three minutes to go in the game, New York led 10–7. A Brady-to-Moss touchdown pass with 2:42 remaining put New England ahead. But the Giants, now trailing 14–10, had a miracle left in them. On third down at his own 44, Manning dropped back to pass. The

Patriots' Jarvis Green had Eli firmly in his grasp, but the QB somehow escaped. Manning floated a wobbling ball deep downfield. David Tyree leaped for the ball and pressed it against his helmet. He held it on top of his head even while being tackled for a 32-yard reception. Manning then won the game with a 13-yard touchdown pass to Plaxico Burress with 39 seconds left.

"We came so close to being special," said New England's Richard Seymour. But instead, said New York's Antonio Pierce, "We shocked the world."

The NFL is still waiting for its first 19–0 team.

Head coach Bill Belichick pats Tom Brady after another New England victory. This dynamic duo has won four Super Bowls together, but not during the 2007 season.

cerebral Thoughtful and intelligent.

comeback victory A win achieved after a team is losing a game.

completion percentage An equation; passing completions divided by passing attempts.

First Team All-Pro Someone who is voted as the best player in the NFL at his position at the conclusion of the season; several organizations pick all-pro teams, most notably the Associated Press.

fundamentals The basic and essential aspects.

NFL MVP Award An honor presented by several organizations to the NFL's most valuable player; the MVP Award referred to in this book is the one presented by the Associated Press.

passer rating A complicated formula meant to rate a quarterback's passing success; it factors in completions, completion percentage, passing yards, touchdown throws, and interceptions.

pigskin Another word for a football, since footballs were once made using the skin of pigs.

pizzazz Excitement, energy, and flair.

point differential The difference between the number of points a team scores and the amount it allows.

Pro Bowl The all-star game for NFL players, held after the season is over (played in Honolulu, Hawaii, since 1980).

workhorse A running back who can be relied on to run the ball a lot each week.

FURTHER READING

Books

Anastasio, Dina. *What Is the Super Bowl?* New York, NY: Grosset & Dunlap, 2015.

Gilbert, Sara. *The Story of the Green Bay Packers.* Mankato, MN: Creative Education, 2014.

Graves, Will. *The Best NFL Offenses of All Time.* Edina, MN: ABDO Publishing, 2014.

Stewart, Mark. *The Pittsburgh Steelers.* Chicago, IL: Norwood House Press, 2013.

Whiting, Jim. *The Story of the New England Patriots.* Creative Education, 2014.

Websites

NFL Rush

nflrush.com

Includes kid-oriented NFL stories, word games, quizzes, computer games, and tons of other fun stuff.

NFL Zone

sikids.com/nfl-zone

Sports Illustrated for Kids offers NFL stories that kids will enjoy, plus a "Cool Stuff" section, "Kid Reporter," and more.

Pro-Football-Reference.com

pro-football-reference.com

Includes statistics on every player in NFL history.

INDEX